101 Jokes For Grammar Nerds

Elias Hill

Illustrations By: Katherine Hogan

Please write "before" instead of "B4".

We use English, not Bingo.

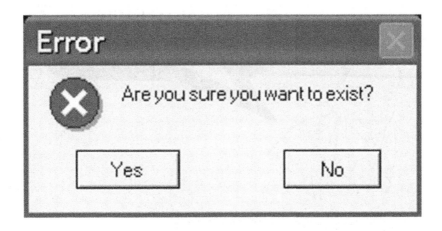

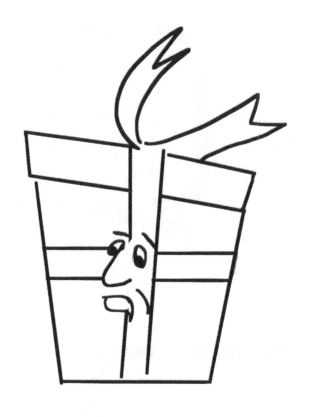

The present tense, or the tense present?

If you have nothing grammatically correct to say,

please say nothing at all.

When you spell a word so wrong,

auto-correct just gives you a shrug.

I've had this phone for five years now, and it's really on it's last, legs.

What happened when the semicolon disobeyed the grammar rules?

It was given two consecutive sentences.

**EMPLOYEES
MUST WASH THEIR
HANDS BEFORE LIVING**

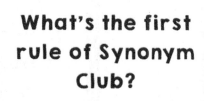

Did you hear the one about the woman who went into labor and started shouting, "Shouldn't! Wouldn't! Couldn't" and "Can't"?

She was having contractions.

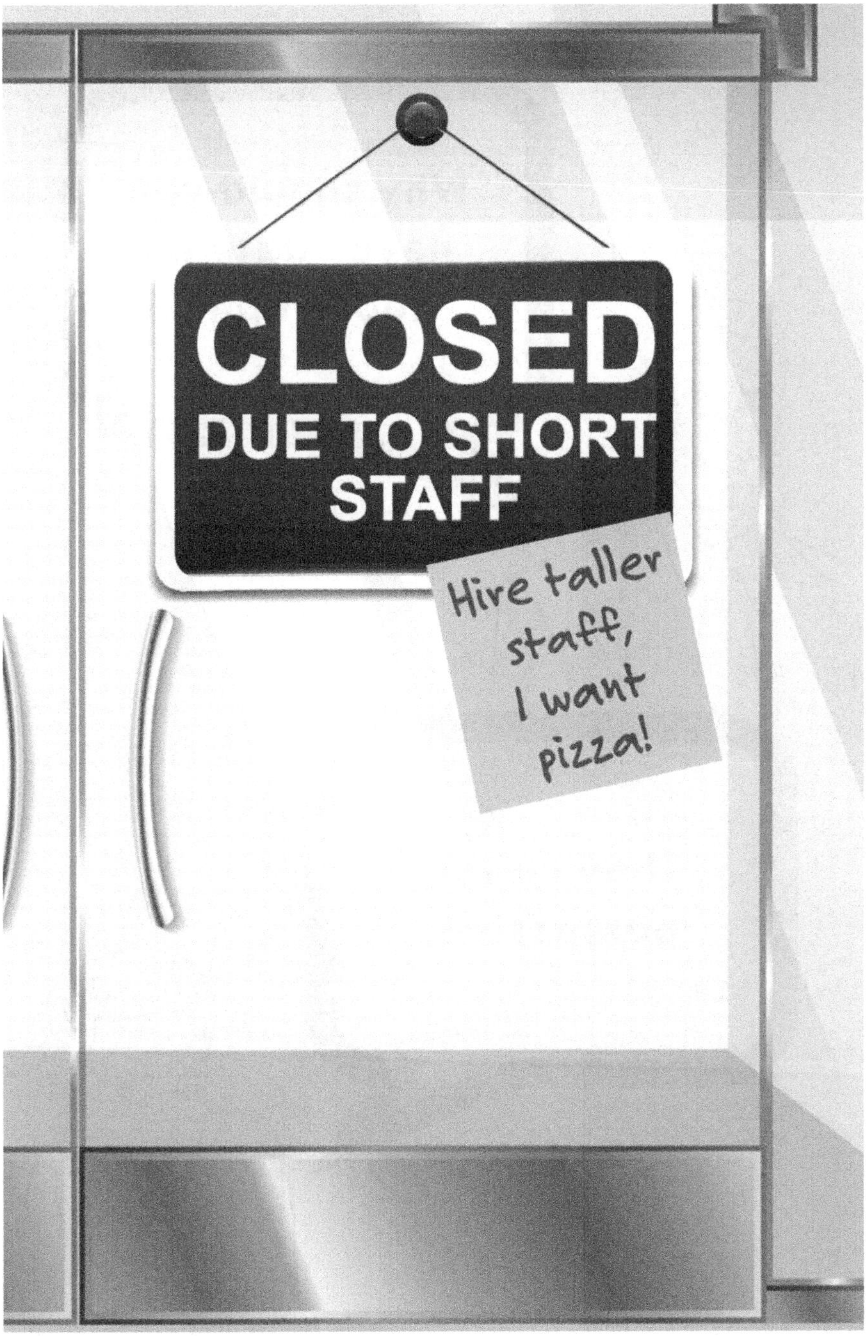
CLOSED
DUE TO SHORT
STAFF
Hire taller
staff,
I want
pizza!

What did the librarian think of the prison library?

It had its prose and cons.

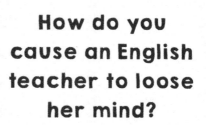

How do you cause an English teacher to loose her mind?

See above.

My life is a constant battle between wanting to correct grammar,
and wanting to keep my friends.

Never leave alphabet soup on the stove and then go out.

It could spell disaster.

I compulsively check and recheck my writing out of fear of publishing online typos.

Hello, my name is Brian and I'm a typochondriac.

"That's what."

        - She

Some days I wish I never graduated middle school,

so your grammar wouldn't bother me so much.

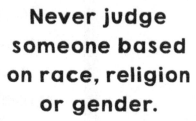

Never judge someone based on race, religion or gender.

Only judge someone based on grammar, spelling and proper sentence structure.

How many crime story writers does it take to change a light bulb?

Two. One to screw the bulb almost all the way in, and one to deliver a twist ending.

An independent variable is

a variable that doesn't need another variable to buy it things.

> What's the longest word in the English language?

> "Smiles," because it has a mile between its first and last letters.

Bad grammar make
me [sic].

Remember, if you're losing an argument,

just start correcting their grammar.

A police officer knocked on my door complaining my dog was chasing a boy on a bike.

"That's impossible," I said, "my dog doesn't even own a bike!"

I wonder what people who type "4" instead of "for"

do with all their free time?

If the English language made any sense,

"catastrophe" would be an apostrophe with fur.

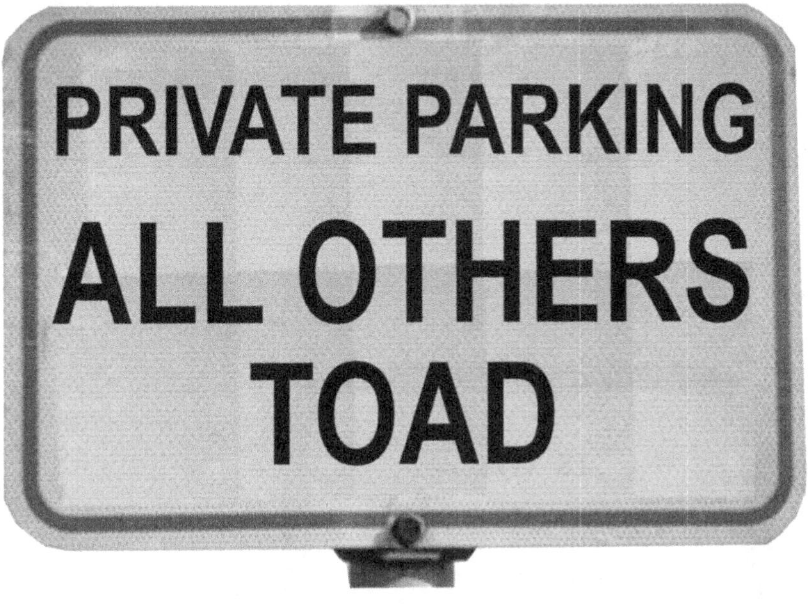
PRIVATE PARKING
ALL OTHERS
TOAD

Writing "etc.",

is the equivalent of saying your brain gives up.

I hate that moment when I spell a common word correctly,

but it looks so wrong I stare at it forever.

himself

That one
is so reflexive,
he just does
things out
of habit.

She we

If I ever text "your" instead of "you're" or "accept" instead of "except",

I've been kidnapped and am signaling for help.

Meet me in
the executive
bored room

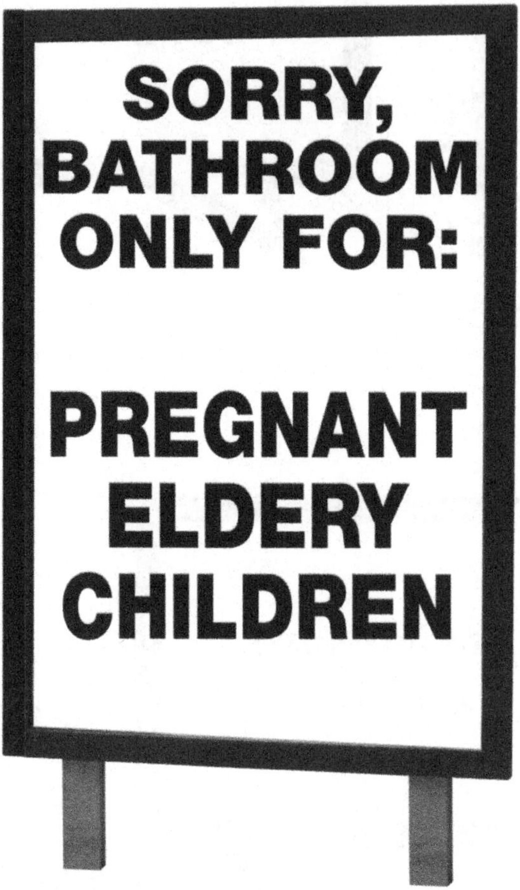
SORRY,
BATHROOM
ONLY FOR:
PREGNANT
ELDERY
CHILDREN

A word in this sentence is misspelled. What is the word?

"Misspelled".

What does your grandpa do?

He don't do nothing.

Your grammar!

Oh, she don't do nothing either.

Made in the USA
Monee, IL
11 December 2021

84781446R00059